Celtic Mythology

Religion of The
Iron Age Celts

Table of Contents

Introduction 1

Chapter One: Dagda 9

Chapter Two: Morrigan 17

Chapter Three: Lugh 24

Chapter Four: Cu Chulainn 36

Chapter Five: Other Important Celtic Gods........... 49

Conclusion.. 69

References 72

Introduction

Celtic mythology is one of the most ancient mythologies in the European continent. Celtic mythology is replete with magic, adventure, romance, and heroism. The Celts were a powerful set of people who populated and dominated a large part of Europe from around 1000 BC until about 225 BC when they faced their first defeat against the Romans.

After the Roman invasions, the Celtic people were reduced to a small number of groups, and yet interestingly, their mythology survived and continues to do so. The Celtic mythological stories were passed on through the generations in oral form until the Medieval Period when, thanks to a few Welsh and Irish monks, they got written down and recorded never to be lost to humankind.

At the peak of power, the Celts dominated a significant portion of Europe. Their geographical clout extended from the British Isles in the West to present-day Turkey in the East. The resourceful and naturally rich regions of Italy, Macedonia, Delphi, and Rome were under the control of the Celts.

Interestingly, before they defeated the Celts, the Romans are known to have had immense respect and fear for the Celts, thanks to their reputation of being courageous and fierce warriors. But, by 84 AD, the Celts had lost most of Britain to the Romans. Simultaneously, Germanic tribes defeated the Celts in the Central European regions.

Only a few regions, including some parts of northern Britain and Ireland, remained free of Roman dominance. The Celts in this region passed on Celtic culture, traditions, and their mythology through generations. Six Celtic groups survive to this day, and these groups include people from Scotland, Ireland, Brittany, Wales, the Isle of Man, and Cornwall.

It is vital to remember that the ancient Celts did not belong to one particular nation or race. They were not ruled by a centralized government. They did not build great cities and towns. They were simple, hardy people who lived off the land. However, they did construction hill forts, quite likely from the point of view defending themselves from invasions.

The Celts were a varied set of people from different geographies across Europe who were bound together by Celtic traditions, culture, language, and customs. By around 100 BC, many large groups of Celts started settlements in certain areas for the convenience of trading with one another.

These Celtic settlements had a clear-cut, hierarchical social structure with the king taking the top stop. A king ruled over a particular tribe or group of people. Each tribe had three distinct classes of people, including:

1. The noble warriors and knights
2. The Druids or the religious priests
3. The commoners including farmers, traders, and others

The Druids came from noble families and were highly regarded and respected in the tribe. In addition to performing priestly functions, the Druids were advisers, teachers, and judges. Moreover, the tribespeople treated their Druids warily because they were believed to have magical powers as well.

Much of our present-day knowledge on Celtic mythology is based on writings and manuscripts recorded by Irish and Welsh monks during the Medieval Period. This was thought to have lasted from 500 AD to about 1500 AD. The Irish accounts date from around 700 AD while the Welsh accounts date from around 1300 AD. Many of these medieval manuscripts recount numerous legends and myths of the ancient Celts.

Two of the most important sources of Celtic mythology are:

- The Mabinogion is the earliest collection of prose and poetry of British literature. These stories are believed to have been compiled by Welsh monks between the 12th and 13th centuries.

- Cath Maige Tuired is the collective name given to two epic texts that speak of the First and Second Battle of Moytura.

A wide variety of magical characters, shape-changing animals, and supernatural beings appear in Celtic mythology. However, most of these characters were locally idolized deities with special powers as opposed to gods and goddesses. Every tribe had its own local deity who protected and looked after the welfare of the tribespeople. Interestingly, many of these local deities across different tribes had similar characteristic traits.

Also, some of the deities were more important and significant than others. For example, Lugus, or Lug, is the sun god and is associated with war, arts, and healing. Another important deity was Cernunnos, the horned god who was associated with fertility and animals.

There was no dearth of female deities in Celtic mythology. For example, Morrigan or the Great Queen was a moniker to describe three female deities, including Morrigan, Badb, and Nemain, all being war goddesses. The three of them would appear as ravens during battles.

Two more important female deities were Brigit, the goddess of healing, learning, and metalworking, and Epona, the horse-goddess who was associated with death, fertility, and water.

An important element found right through Celtic mythology is the 'cauldron.' There were magic cauldrons for a lot of things. There was the cauldron of plenty that provided limitless supplies of food. The cauldron of rebirth, as evidenced by its name, had the power to bring the dead back to life.

Another recurring element found in Celtic mythology is adventurous, dangerous, and mysterious voyages and journeys undertaken by the heroes. Mischief, love, and romance were recurring themes too in Celtic mythology. The larger-than-life heroes went on dangerous missions to complete seemingly impossible tasks in order to marry their lady love. Moreover, the gods and goddesses also played tricks on humans and on each other.

The underworld of the Celts was unique too. Here, there was no death, and there was no work to do too. The spirits and gods who lived in the Celtic underworld never got old. Human beings could get access to this enchanted place through various 'portals.'

For example, humans could enter the underworld via burial mounds called sidhe, lakes, mountains, caves, etc. Humans could also choose to complete a perilous journey to reach the underworld. Once they reached the underworld, they could live happily ever after! So, it is easy to imagine the rich color and intricate tapestry Celtic mythology wove in our minds. So, go on and read to find out more about the different heroes, gods, and goddesses who adorn Celtic mythology.

Celtic mythology is categorized into four cycles, namely:

- **Mythological Cycle** - This cycle focuses on stories that give detailed accounts of various invasions of Ireland by supernatural beings, deities, and others. This set of tales was primarily about Tuatha De Dannan. The main source of the stories contained in the Mythological Cycle is the "Book of Invasions" or Labor Gabala Erenn.

- **Fenian Cycle** - This cycle focuses on the theme of hunting. In this cycle, stories are woven around a group of heroes led by Fionn mac Cumhaill who protect the Celtic lands.

- **Ultonian or the Ulster Cycle** - This set of stories is focused on the tribe of Ulaidh or Ulster and its heroes and warriors.

- **Kings Cycle** - Also known as the Historical Cycle, this series of tales and myths are centered around Celtic kings.

Chapter One:

Dagda

Dagda was the chief of the Irish tribe Tuatha de Danann which translates of "tribe of Danu." We get the information about Tuatha de Danann from Lebor Gabála Érenn, a collection of Irish prose and poetry. Known as the 'Book of Invasions" in English, this collection of narratives in the Irish language is intended as the history of Ireland and the Irish people.

According to Lebor Gabála Érenn, Tuatha de Danann was the fifth of the six groups of settlers who arrived in mythical Ireland with their chief, Dagda. Although he did not hold the title of king, Dagda was highly revered by the people of his tribe and was consulted for everything as if he was the king.

The people of this tribe originated from four different cities in the north of the Emerald Isle. Including Murias, Farias, Findias, and Gorias. These people were already well-learned in arts and sciences and magic when they landed in Ireland. Dagda was the god of life and death, fertility, Druidry, and agriculture. A master of druid magic, Dagda was a sought-after advisor too. There were many stories regarding Dagda's parentage.

According to one tale, Dagda's parents were Elatha and Ethniu, the daughter of King Balor. Other tales speak of Badurn being the father of Dagda. Many tales speak of his two brothers, namely Nuada, the king of gods, and Oghma, a great Celtic hero and champion.

Many Celtic myths represented the three brothers living together in a triumvirate with Dagda as the advisor or chief, Nuada as the king, and Oghma as the champion. Also, Dagda and his brothers are sometimes represented as one god in three persons because often, the three brothers shared similar attributes and were referred to as king or chief simultaneously.

Dagda's primary place of residence was in Brú na Bóinne. This place exists even today and consists of a series of Neolithic mounds in County Meath. These mounds, found on the banks of the

River Boyne, are believed to have been constructed around 3200 BC and experts opine that they are older than the more famous ancient landmarks like the Stonehenge or the Great Pyramid of Egypt.

One of the mounds called Newgrange is believed to be in perfect alignment with the rising sun during the winter solstice. The Newgrange mound is believed to represent Dagda's control over the seasons as well as his power on day and night.

He possessed three magical tools or sacred relics, including:

A magic cauldron – The 'coire ansic' or cauldron of plenty had a limitless supply of bountiful feasts to offer anyone who came to Dagda. Crafted in Murias, one of the four islands from which the Tuatha De Dannan originated, this magical cauldron was one of the Four Jewels or Treasures of the tribe, the other three beings:

- The stone of destiny - Referred to as Lia Fail, the stone of destiny was believed to have been brought from the island of Farias. It was set up on the Hill of Tara on which the

High Kings of Ireland were crowned and lived.

- Sword of Lugh - Also called the "spear of victory," this sword came from the island of Findias. The longer it was used, the hotter it became. At night, it was stored in a vat of water to prevent it from scorching the earth.

- Sword of Nuada - Sometimes called the "Shining Sword," this was made in Gorias and brought to Ireland by King Nuada.

A magical harp – Called 'uaithne' in the Celtic language, Dagda used his magical harp to control:

- The seasons and bring them to order.

- The emotions of people to get them to do the right thing

The power to control and bring order to everything and everyone rendered by the magical harp also gave Dagda the title of "god of order."

A gigantic club - Called 'lorg mór,' Dagda's mighty club had the power to take and grant life. One single swing of the club can slay nine men. Also, a mere touch of the club could revive the dead.

Dagda also had two magical pigs, one of which was always growing, and the other was always roasting. He also had a magical orchard in which sweet fruit grew perennially.

Dagda was described as a gigantic figure with ill-fitting clothes that always managed to expose his buttocks and stomach. Despite the sad state of his garb and his oafish appearance, Dagda was revered for his wit, wisdom, and wile. He was extraordinarily powerful and had multiple magic tricks up his sleeve.

Other titles used for Dagda are:

- Ochaid Ollathair - Horseman or All-Father
- Fer Benn - the Horned Man
- Ruad Rofhessa - Lord of Great Knowledge
- Dáire - the Fertile One
- Cerrce - Striker

He was the foremost ancient Irish gods and was called the "great god," and the 'great' reflected his outstanding mastery over multiple skills rather than his personality or character. He was so powerful that he could command the seasons with a simple strum of his harp. Since Dagda was also a druid, he had mastery and control over mystical and magical things too.

So, why the gruff appearance? Some scholars opine that this gruff, almost-comical appearance, was added by the Irish monks when they recorded Celtic mythology in the Medieval Period, perhaps with the intention of making Celtic gods appear comical and foolish in front of their own deity.

But, it must be noted that despite the appearance was comical, Dagda was represented as a wise, powerful, and witty man with skills that covered a wide range of subjects including art, Druidry, and military strategy.

Being the chief of his tribe, Dagda had many lovers and fathered numerous children. Some of his children who went on to become Celtic heroes include Aengus, Midir, and Brigid. His most important lovers include Morrigan, who was also his wife, and Boann, the river goddess.

Dagda and Boann's love story is quite unique. The river goddess was already married to Elcmar, a judge of Tuatha de Dannon, when Dagda fell for her. Dagda hatched a plan to court Boann. He sent

Elcmar away on an errand to King Bres. Boann got pregnant when her husband was away.

To prevent retribution of any kind either to his lover and his child, Dagda used his magical powers to hold the sun in its place for the entire period of Boann's pregnancy. This allowed Boann to carry and deliver Dagda's child in a single day. This child, Aengus, who went on to become the Celtic god of love and poetry, was brought up by Midir, another son of Dagda.

When Dagda arrived in Ireland with his tribespeople, he had to conquer and defeat the settlers who came before them, the most powerful tribe being the Fomorians. The Fomorians were a monster race, and they were ruled by King Balor, who was infamous for his cruelty. He was itching to gain control over Ireland again. Dagda knew that his tribe had no choice but to battle with the Fomorians if they wanted to consolidate power in Ireland.

He planned the battle very carefully. Using his tricks and magic, he first ensured that the Fomorians' resources, including their sheep, were taken away. His wife Morrigan, the goddess of death and battle, prophesied that Tuatha de Danann would be victorious over the Fomorians, but there would be a price to pay.

The two forces met at Moytura, where the fierce fight for control over Ireland was fought between Dagda's Tuatha de Danann and King Balor's Fomorians. In this battle, Dagda's brother and King Balor laid low. King Balor's wife, Cethlenn, participated in the battle, and in fact, mortally wounded Dagda. His magical harp was also stolen, although it was recovered later on.

Dagda returned to his dwelling place in Brú na Bóinne, where he breathed his last, succumbing to his battle injuries. He was laid to rest in the mounds. Dagda had ruled over Ireland for over 70-80 years.

Deities like the Irish Dagda are also found outside Ireland. Powerful gods wielding cauldrons and clubs were found all over Great Britain and France. For example, the Celtic god Secullus, worshipped by the Gauls as the god of agriculture, carried a hammer, barrel (in some stories, it was a cup instead of a barrel).

Chapter Two:

Morrigan

Morrigan was the fearful "Phantom Queen" or "Great Queen," the Irish goddess of death, war, and discord. She was represented as a single entity as well as three sisters with the power to foretell the deaths of kings and worries and issue other such terrifying prophecies. Her title of the "Phantom Queen" is representative of her connection with the dead.

The Morrigan appeared before great battles and would offer prophecy to gods, kings, and warriors. She flew around the battlefield as a congress of ravens to carry away the dead warriors. She was married to Dagda, the chief of Tuatha da Dannon. Her husband also came to her for prophecies.

Morrigan was primarily the Irish goddess of death and war, and also the goddess of fate and prophecy. She was considered to be an all-knowing goddess and was willing to share her knowledge for a price. She used poetry rather than prose to make prophecies, which, by the way, were always correct and accurate.

Her appearance as a raven to a king or the warriors of a particular side means she favored this side to win. The raven was not the only form she took. She was a shape-shifting goddess and could appear in different forms within the same tale. The most common forms Morrigan took were a warrior-queen, a beautiful maiden, an old crone, and of course, a raven. However, she could shift her shape to the form of other animals, too though she didn't use them frequently.

Morrigan's mother was Ernmas, another Irish mother-goddess who herself was the child of Nuada, the king of Tuatha Dé Danann. Morrigan's father's name is not mentioned in Celtic mythology. She had five siblings, including:

- Sisters Ériu, Banba, and Fódla, who made up the triple deity of the sovereignty and spirit of Ireland.

- Sisters Machs and Badh, who along with Morrigan, formed the triple deity of war and death.

- Brothers Glon, Coscar, Gnim, Ollom, and Fiacha.

- Morrigan is associated with many natural and sacred sites all across Ireland. Some of the important sacred places in Ireland connected with Morrigan include:

- Fulacht na Mór Ríoghna or "cooking pit of the Morrígan" in County Tipperary - this place is believed to have been in existence since the Bronze Age and is also connected with a band of wandering warriors.

- Dá Chich na Morrigna or "two breasts" - this location in County Meath has two hills, which are believed to be "two breasts" of Morrigan. This site could have been used to perform rituals.

The most prominent character trait of Morrigan is that she had the personality and nature of three different goddesses. In many mythological tales, Morrigan appeared both as a single entity as well as three different goddesses operating under the single title of Morrigan.

These three goddesses are not consistent across the various sources of Celtic mythology. Some believe that Morrigan was the name given to the threesome comprising of Badb, Macha, and Anand, the three daughters of Ernmas. Some other sources cite Morrigan to be the sister of Badb and Macha, and the three together were given the title of Morrigan. In this version, Anand was merely another name for Morrigan. All these inconsistent theories created by the Medieval Irish monks perhaps reflect the numerous and confusing sources of Morrigan's origin as passed down orally through generations of the Celts.

Morrigan belonged to the Tuatha De Dannon tribe. When they first arrived in Ireland, they met with resistance from the earlier settlers, primarily the Fomorians and the Firbolgs. The Firbolgs and Tuatha De Dannon forces met at Moytura in County Galway. In this battle, known as the First Battle of Maytura, Morrigan's mother, Ernmas, died, and her grandfather, King Nuada lost a hand. However, the Tuatha De Dannon eventually emerged victorious against the Firbolgs and got a firm footing on Ireland.

Lugh of the Long Arm became the new king of Tuatha De Dannon after Nuada lost his hand in the First Battle of Moytura. King Lugh asked Morrigan to predict the outcome of the war with the Fomorians, who were more formidable than the Firbolgs. As the warriors and the tribespeople of Tuatha De Dannon prepared for the battle with the Fomorians, Dagda went in search of his wife, Morrigan, to prophesy the outcome of the battle.

He found her at the ford of River Unshin in the county of Sligo. Here, the husband and wife made love, after which Morrigan predicted the victory of Tuatha De Dannon in the war with the Fomorians. However, the victory would have a high price attached to it. Also, she told Dagda that she herself would kill Indech, the king of the Fomorians. Further, she would bring the dead king's kidneys and two handfuls of his blood to River Unshin.

The day of the battle dawned, and the Fomorian and Tuatha De Dannon forces faced each other in the Second Battle of Moytura. Morrigan had brought pursuit, death, and destruction to this battle. It is a complete bloodbath. Her husband Dagda, was mortally wounded, and Nuada was killed.

Finally, Morrigan entered the battlefield. She ended the battle, ensuring victory to Tuatha De Danann. The Fomorians were so scared of her prowess that they ran from her and died at sea.

When the battle ended, Morrigan sang a song of celebration. Badb predicted that the world would end when morals decayed, and the sea had no bounty.

Morrigan is more or less unique to Irish mythology; there are some similar characters in other mythologies. For example, Morgan le Fay, the famed antagonist in Arthurian mythology, bears a striking resemblance to Morrigan. Like the Celtic goddess, Morgan was a shapeshifter and soothsayer. Also, Morrigan was similar to Odin of German mythology, considering both of them were connected to ravens, war, and death.

Another important story of Morrigan is connected with Chu Chulainn. A separate chapter is dedicated to this hero. However, Morrigan's part of the hero's story goes as follows:

While Chu Chulainn was busy with back-to-back combats with champions of Connacht in the

Battle Raid of Cooley, Morrigan offered herself to the Ulster hero who rejected her advances, despite being moved by her beauty. Morrigan was furious and decided to avenge what she believed was an insult to her.

She used her shape-shifting powers to transform into an eel and tripped Cu Chulainn as he walked through a ford. He lashed out at the eel and wounded it. She then took the form of a wolf and drove some cattle towards Cu Chulainn. The Ulster warrior used his slingshot and blinded the wolf in one eye. Next, she transformed herself into a cow and led a stampede of cattle towards Cu Chulainn. He fired another shot from his sling, breaking the heifer's leg. This wound forced Morrigan to retreat from the battle with Cu Chulainn.

The rest of Cu Chulainn's story can be found in the chapter dedicated to the unparalleled Ulster warrior.

Chapter Three:

Lugh

This young Irish god was also referred to as Lugh of the Long Arm. He sought revenge for the unjust killing of his father. Known for his all-round skills, Lugh led the Tuatha de Danann to defeat the Fomorians. After Lugh's death, the power and dominance of Tuatha de Danann started to decline.

Lugh of the Long Arm was the Irish god of rulership, kings, and justice. His favorite weapon was the Sleg (or Spear) of Assal, the lightning spear, and he was a master wielder of it. The spear was one of the Four Jewels of Tuatha De Dannan. This spear, which could take the shape of lightning, was impossible to beat in battles. Lugh used two magic words to wield it. He would say 'Ibar' to target and hit the mark, and 'Athibar' to make it come back to him.

In addition to the spear, Lugh possessed and wielded many other weapons too including:

- A boat that could move at considerably high speeds called Sguaba Tuinne, the 'Wind-Sweeper.'

- A powerful slingshot or cloich tabaill, which was immensely useful in the battle against the cruel King Balor of the Fomorians.

- A special sword called Fragarach, which means 'answerer.' This sword was special because it worked like a truth serum. Any person at whom it was pointed could never lie, and he is forced to answer all questions truthfully.

- A special, magical horse called Enbarr of the Flowing Mane, which had the power to travel over land and sea. Lugh also had numerous other horses too.

- A magical greyhound that had the power to turn water into wine. Also, this greyhound called Failinis was invincible in battle and never missed a prey it hunted.

Not only was he a great warrior but also a master of arts and crafts as well as being an excellent trickster. In fact, Lugh is prominently famous for his being a trickster as well as a savior. He lived in Tara in County Meath. The historical High Kings of Ireland lived in Tara. He also had a dwelling in Moytura in County Sligo. Moytura was the place where Lugh became king. His holy day falls on August 1st and is celebrated as Lughnasa.

Although he held many titles, the most common and famous one was 'Lámfada,' or "Of the long arm," a direct reference to the length of his famous spear. Some experts translate the title Lámfada as "Artful Hands," which refers to his great skill in art and craft. His other titles include:

- Ildanach or the Skilled God
- mac Ethnenn or Ethleen or the son of Ethniu or Ethliu, his Fomorian mother
- mac Cien or the son of Cian, his Tuatha De Dannan father
- Macnia or the Youthful Warrior
- Lonnbéimnech or the Fierce Striker
- Conmac, the Son of the Hound

Lugh was also the first Chief Ollam (Ollamh Érenn) of Ireland. This title reflected his multifaceted skills as a ruler, judge, and poet. After his death, the title of Chief Ollam was a ranked position in all Irish courts. Every High King of Ireland had a Chief Ollam, and every king had an ollam who served him in an advisory role.

Lugh of the Long Arm descended from two rival bloodlines. His mother, Ethniu, the daughter of the cruel Fomorian King Balor. His father, Cian, was the son of Dian Cedh, a healer in the Tuatha De Dannon camp. In Cath Maig Tuired, the marriage of Ethniu and Cian was described as a dynastic union between the Fomorians and Tuatha De Dannan.

Another folktale has a more interesting tale of the birth of Lugh. King Balor was warned through a prophecy that his grandson would kill him. To prevent such a mishap, Balor hid his daughter, Ethniu, in an almost inaccessible tower on Tory Island. However, Cian took the help of a fairy woman named Birog, who magically transported him to the tower where Ethniu was imprisoned.

Ethniu and Cian made love, and she became pregnant with his child and gave birth to triplets. Balor discovered the birth of his grandchildren. He gave them to a servant and told her to kill the babies. Two of them were drowned. However, one of the three fell into a safe harbor and was found and rescued by Birog, who handed over the child to Cian. Cian fostered and protected this child.

It is believed that Lugh was brought up by foster parents. There are multiple versions of who his foster-parents were. Some of these versions are:

- Manannan mac Lir, the Irish sea god
- Tailtiu, the Firbolg Queen
- Gavida, the god of the smiths

When Lugh was ready and prepared to enter the court of the king, he came to Tara, the seat of King Nuada of Tuatha De Danann. It was the court policy that anyone wanting to enter the court would have to possess a special skill that he or she can offer a service to the king.

Although Lugh was skilled at various things, he was not allowed to enter the court as the doorkeeper said that the positions for all the skills that Lugh possessed were already filled. Immediately, Lugh asked if the court had a master of all skills to which the doorkeeper replied in the negative. In this way, he got an entry into the court as Chief Ollam or the master of all skills.

King Nuada was very impressed with Lugh and his abilities. Foreseeing his potential to bring salvation to Tuatha De Danann, Nuada made Lugh in charge of the upcoming battle with the Fomorians. However, before the battle with the Fomorians happened, the First Battle of Moytura between Tuatha De Dannon and Firbolgs took place in which King Nuada lost a hand. He was then forced to give up the throne in accordance with the tribal traditions, which mandated that a king cannot have any blemishes. Bres, a half-Fomorian, became the king of Tuatha De Danann, and he delayed the war with Fomorians.

In the meantime, Lugh's father Cian, was killed by Tuireann's sons Brian, Iuchar, and Iucharba. Tuireann was an arch-enemy of Cian. The three sons located Cian and transformed him into a pig and slaughtered him. But, just before he was slaughtered, Cian managed to change back to his human form, an act necessary to give his heir the right to seek revenge for his death.

Tuireann's sons tried to bury Cian's body two times before they were caught in the act. However, both times, the ground opened up and spat out the body of Cian. After the third attempt, Lugh came upon the grave and found out that it was the grave of his father who had been slain unjustly. Lugh was devastated by the death of his father. He began to plot revenge against his father's killers.

Lugh threw a grand feast and invited Tuireann's sons to it. He asked them what they would do to someone who murdered their father. They said that killing the murderer would be the right thing to do. At this point, Lugh revealed his true identity and said as he was Cian's heir, killing the three of them for murdering his father would also be the right thing to do.

Lugh set them a series of dangerous missions for Tuireann's sons to perform. The three sons were able to successfully complete all but the final mission. Knowing and accepting that the last mission was impossible to complete, Tuireann begged for mercy and asked that his sons be spared. But Lugh was relentless in his thirst for revenge.

The sons of Tuireann were mortally wounded while they tried to complete the final task, and as Lugh withheld the magical pigskin that had the power to heal their wounds, Tuireann's sons died. Tuireann died in grief, following the death of his sons, and Lugh got justice for his father's murder.

Lugh was a master of multiple skills. Being the god of oaths gave him control over rulers and other noblemen. He served as a judge in many forms. His judgments were all swift and merciless. Interestingly, despite his merciless attitude towards crime, Lugh himself was a trickster who would happily lie, steal, and cheat to defeat his opponents.

With his father from Tuatha De Dannan and his mother from Fomorian lineage, Lugh had a unique heritage. He is also believed to have invented many games, including athletics, horse-racing, and fidchell, the Irish version of chess.

Lugh had many lovers and wives, the most important ones being Nas, Bui, and Buach. Nas was the daughter of the King of Britain who bore Lugh his son, Ibic. However, the most famous son of Lugh, Cu Chulainn, was borne by the mortal Deichtine. Cu Chulainn was one of the most popular heroes of the Ulster Cycle. A separate chapter in this book is dedicated to Cu Chulainn.

When Bres became king of Tuatha De Dannan, he openly supported the Fomorians by forcing Tuatha De Danann to pay tribute to them and work as their slaves. Lugh's grandfather, Nuada, decided it was time to get rid of King Bres. He got himself a silver hand first and then a handmade of flesh, which eliminated his blemish, and he was able to become king again. Bres was exiled, and the war was declared on the Fomorians.

The Fomorian and Tuatha De Danann forces met at Moytura in County Sligo and fought each other in what was called the Second Battle of Moytura. Lugh of the Long Arm fought ferociously on behalf of Tuatha De Danann using both his Assal spear and his slingshot.

Lugh's maternal grandfather, King Balor, slew King Nuada in this battle. At this instant, Lugh used his slingshot to shoot a stone at King Balor's eyes, and he fell down dead too. Balor's death turned the tide in favor of Tuatha De Danann. The Fomorians were defeated and were pushed into the sea. Lugh of the Long Arm was named king of Tuatha De Danann.

After the defeat of the Fomorians, Bres was brought before Lugh. Bres begged for mercy, and this time, he chose to forgive Bres, provided he teaches the tribespeople of Tuatha De Danann how to plow the land. Bres had no choice but to agree to this proposal. Finally, Lugh ruled over a united Ireland.

Of course, the people of Tuatha De Danann, including Lugh, could never really forget or forgive Bres for what he did to them when he was king. So, as soon as he finished teaching everything about farming and plowing the land, they wanted to kill him. Lugh crafted 300 beautiful wooden cows and filled up with deliciously-looking but poisonous red milk. He offered these to Bres, who couldn't refuse such generosity. He drank up all the milk and fell dead.

Lugh's death was similar to what he did to avenge his father's death. His wife, Buach, had a love affair with Cermait, son of Dagda. When Lugh got to know of this, he got Cermait killed. However, Cermait's three sons vowed revenge. They captured the king of Tuatha De Danann and drowned him in a lake which became famous as Loch Lugborta, a famous water body that exists even today in County Westmeath, Ireland.

Lugh had ruled over Tuatha De Danann for more than 40 years, and after his death, the decline of his tribe set in. Lugh lived in Tír na nÓg or "Land of the Young," one of the underworld regions in Celtic mythology. He appeared in the mortal regularly. It was during one of his journeys to the mortal when he met with and made love to Deichtine, a mortal, and his famous son, Cu Chulainn was born. Lugh appeared to his son, later on, to heal his wounds in a battle.

Lugh was a prominent Celtic god character who appeared in European tribes as well as Britain as Lugus. In Wales, he was known as Llew Llaw Gyffes. Often, his name appeared with his famous title, "Of the Long Arm," in these regions as well. In addition to being the god of rulership and master of all skills, Lugh was also connected with the sun and light.

Lugh's character was very similar to that of Freyr, the Norse god of fertility, who also had a boat that could change in size depending on the need. Also, Freyr's father was Njord, the Norse god of the sea, just like Lugh's father was Manannan mac Lir, the Celtic god of the sea.

In addition to Loch Lugborta, multiple sites across Europe bear the name of Lugh of the Long Arm. In Ireland, the most significant one is Louth, the village in the heart of County Louth that is named after him.

Lughnasadh, the Irish harvest festival which falls on August 1st is dedicated to Lugh. It is celebrated across Ireland, Scotland, and the Isle of Man. August 1st marks the day Lugh defeated the spirits of Tír na nÓg, the Celtic underworld. Lugh celebrated his victory by setting in the fruit-harvest time early. He also hosted games and sports in memory of Tailtiu, his foster-mother.

Lughnasadh is celebrated even today. It has various Christian names, including "Mountain Sunday" and "Garland Sunday." Many revelers celebrate this festival by climbing hills and mountains.

Chapter Four:

Cu Chulainn

O ne of the most famous heroes of the Ulster Cycle, Cu Chulainn, possessed outstanding warrior skills and was extremely passionate. He was able to channelize the power of his unparalleled rage to decimate hordes of enemies. The son of Lugh of the Long Arm, Cu Chulainn, was the Irish champion of the Ulster Kingdom. His passions ran deep, and even though his sorrows were many, he is the best known Celtic mythological hero even today in Ireland.

Cu Chulainn, which translates of "Hound of Culann " is spelled in multiple ways, including Cúailnge, Cúchulain, and Cú Chulaind. Although Cu Chulainn was a title, this name was used far more often than his birth name, which was Sétanta, meaning "son of Sualtam," after his mortal father. Another famous nickname of his was "the Hound of Ulster," which reflected his unstinting loyalty to the Ulster Cycle and his title.

Even though he is believed to have been born in Dundalk, Cu Chulainn made Ulster as his home. He defended his home with unflinching loyalty and remained the undying symbol of Ulster, the nine-county northern Ireland province, to this day.

Cu Chulainn's primary claim to fame was his outstanding warrior skills. Right from his childhood, he underwent training in Scotland and Ireland to become a warrior and a killing machine. Not only were his skills unmatched, but also he was one of the very few warriors who could take on multiple opponents simultaneously and be victorious over them. His physical and mental strength was so great that he could easily wear off a sleeping potion in just an hour as against ordinary men who would need an entire day to sleep off the same potion.

Cu Chulainn's biggest weapon on the battlefield was his warrior rage or ríastrad. His rage was so powerful that he could go berserk, killing both friends and enemies relentlessly. His friends had to take extreme measures and go to great lengths to calm down his extraordinary rage.

Many magical elements powered cu Chulainn's indomitable strength, including:

- The magnificent horses named Liath Macha and Dub Sainglend that drew his chariot. Liath Macha was referred to as the "king of horses."

- Gáe Bulg, also referred to as gai-bulga, or gae-bolga, a powerful spear made with the bones of Curruid, a sea monster, whose carcass was found on the seashore. The spear was given to him by Aife after he defeated her in single combat.

- The protection of two geas or magical taboos which, if broken, would affect his strength and increase his vulnerability to mortality. The two geas were that Cu Chulainn should never reject the hospitality of a woman, and he should never eat dog meat.

Cu Chulainn was a very good-looking man with color-changing magical hair. However, different sources also describe the color of his hair as being blonde, red, or black.

Cu Chulainn's mother was Deichtine of Ulster, and his father was Lugh of the Long Arm. There is an interesting story of his birth because Deichtine was actually betrothed to Sualtam mac Róich.

One day, Deichtine and her father, the king of Ulster, Conchobar mac Nessa, went on a hunting expedition. A fierce snowstorm forced the father-daughter duo to take shelter in a grand palace.

There, Deichtine saw a pregnant woman who needed help with the delivery of her baby. Deichtine was happy to help, and a baby boy was born. When Deichtine and her father woke up the next morning, they found themselves in Brú na Bóinne and not in the palace where they had taken refuge last night. Also, the baby died as there was no one to take care of it.

Lugh of the Long Arm who was residing in Tír na nÓg, the Celtic underworld appeared before Deichtine and told her that the child was his, and he was now growing in her belly. Soon after her marriage, she delivered a child whom she named Setanta as Lugh of the Long Arm wanted. Setanta was brought up by his maternal grandfather.

However, some of the sources have varied ideas on his father's identity. But the most famous and accepted tale is that he was the son of the immortal Lugh of the Long Arm, and his mortal father was Sualtam mac Róich. Also, as you already know, his maternal grandfather, Conchobar mac Nessa, was the king of Ulster.

Setanta had an outstanding childhood. Thanks to his power and strength, even as a young boy, he always wanted to join the famous boy-troop in Emain Macha, present-day Navan Fort in County Armagh. When he was just six years old, he set out on his own to become a member of this rather fierce boy-troop. He walked into the playing field belonging to this group, where none would dare take a step without seeking protection first.

The members of this gang saw Setanta's act of walking into their arena without seeking protection as a challenge and charged towards the young boy. However, Setanta easily beat all the boys single-handedly. In fact, Setanta became so ferocious that King Conchobar had to come and stop the fight. From that day onwards, the boy-troop swore allegiance to Setanta.

The story of how Setanta became Cu Chulainn or the Hound of Culann is also interesting. Once, Culann, a famous smith in Ulster, invites his king, Conchobar, for dinner. Conchobar extends the invitation to Setanta as well. Setanta said he would join him a little later for dinner.

However, Conchobar forgets to tell Culann that Setanta would join them later. So, when the young boy set foot in Culann's home, Culann set loose his ferocious hound on him, thinking that an intruder had come in. Chu Chulainn killed the guard hound in self-defense.

However, Culann was so upset at the death of his favorite hound that Setanta promised to rear and train another hound for the smith. He further promised that he himself would guard Culann's home until the hound was trained and ready. This act earned Setanta the title of Chu Chulainn or the "hound of Culann."

One day, when he was seven years old, Cu Chulainn overheard a druid named Cathbad telling his students that anyone who that particular day would become the greatest warrior in his lifetime. Cu Chulainn went to King Conchobar and requested to try some weapons from the king's arsenal.

But, none of the weapons could stand the strength of seven-year-old Cu Chulainn. Finally, Conchobar allowed the boy warrior to take up his own powerful arms.

Unfortunately, Cu Chulainn did not hear Cathbad's entire prophecy, which was the person who took up arms on that day would become the greatest warrior of his times but will have a very short life.

Cu Chulainn was then sent to train under Scáthach, the famous warrior-queen of Scotland. There, he encountered Aife, Scathachs' rival, and twin sister. After besting her in one-to-one combat, Cu Chulainn had a relationship with Aife, and she got pregnant with his son, Connla. After his training, Cu Chulainn returned to Ireland and married Emer, daughter of Forgall Monach, another Ulster warrior. Incidentally, Cu Chulainn kills his own son, Connla, a few years later, mistaking him to be an intruder trying to get into Conchobar's fort.

Considering his amazing looks and beauty, Cu Chulainn is believed to have left behind a string of broken hearts, including Fand, the wife of Manannán mac Lir, the Celtic sea god. Some tales also talk of his relationship with Ferdiad, his warrior companion.

Cu Chulainn's most famous battle was the Battle Raid of Cooley. The Ulster Kingdom had a powerful and strong stud bull that was the secret of the kingdom's power and riches. This stud bull called Donn Cúailnge or the Bull of Cooley had a twin that belonged to the husband of Medb, the Queen of Connacht. Medb wanted to steal the Bull of Cooley to equal the wealth and power of her husband. So, she attacks Ulster.

An age-old curse temporarily disables the warriors of Ulster. According to this curse, the Ulster warriors would experience labor pains just when they need to go for an important battle. The curse comes into play, and none of the Ulster warriors can battle the Connacht champions, except Cu Chulainn, who is exempt from the curse.

Cu Chulainn is so powerful and strong that he is able to fend off Connacht's army. He challenges the Connacht champions to single combat and wins against each of his combatants with ease. When he rested for a while during the battle, Morrigan, in the form of beautiful approaches him and offers herself to him.

He rejects her and earns her wrath. Morrigan tries to hinder him in the battle three times. Each time, she herself is wounded. Later on, Cu Chulainn himself helps Morrigan heal her wounds. You can read this story in detail in the chapter dedicated to Morrigan after she is healed. Morrigan reveals herself to Cu Chulainn and prophesies that Cu Chulainn will die young, and she herself will be there to witness his death.

The Cattle Raid of Cooley raged on, and Cu Chulainn continued fighting relentlessly despite his exhaustion and wounds. In the battle, he met Fergus mac Róic, his foster-father, who was now exiled. They made a pact with each other that if Cu Chulainn did not fight with them at that point, then Cu Chulainn can call in the same favor whenever Cu Chulainn wanted.

The warriors of Ulster were still not free from the curse and were writhing in the agony of labor pains. Cu Chulainn was getting tired and needed to take a break to refresh himself. At this point, the boy-troop from Emain Macha led by Ferdiad, Cu Chulainn's brother-in-arms, comes to his help. These warriors take on the champions of Connacht, giving Cu Chulainn a much-needed break.

As Cu Chulainn slept for a while, he had a dream in which he met his father, Lugh of the Long

Arm. He wakes up, feeling completely refreshed and ready to battle again. When he returns to the battlefield, he sees that all the loyal warriors of the boy-troop of Emain Macha, including Ferdiad, are killed by the Connacht champions.

He gets so angry at the sight of his warrior-friends' bodies that he gets into one of his famous blood-rages. He slaughters so many of the Connacht champions and warriors that he creates a wall of corpses with them. Finally, the Ulster warriors are released from the curse, and all of them join the battle.

Medb knew that the chances of winning against Ulster were slim. So she is forced to retreat. Cu Chulainn gave chase to Medb and was just about to fight her in single combat when he notices that she was in menstruation. In respect of her state, he chooses not to fight with Medb. Instead, he helps to defend her army from the offensive attacks of the Ulster warriors so that she could retreat in dignity.

In this way, Cu Chulainn almost single-handedly secured and protected the revered and all-important stud bull of Cooley. Just as Cathbad had prophesied, Cu Chulainn became the greatest and fiercest warrior in all of Ireland at that time at the tender age of 18.

Considering the young man's power and rage, it was easy for Cu Chulainn to get himself to a lot of enemies, many of them far more powerful than Medb. During one of his various war sojourns, Cu Chulainn had met with and befriended a magical figure. While they started off as friends, they ended up as rivals as they fought over a woman, and Cu Chulainn ended up slaying this person. Lugaid mac Cú Roí was the son of this magical figure, and he was seeking revenge for the death of his father.

First, Lugaid got himself three deadly spears that were powerful enough to slay a king. Then, he plotted with other enemies of Cu Chulainn, including Queen Medb of Connacht. All the rivals of Cu Chulainn agreed that Lugaid's spears offered them the best chance of killing the Ulster hero.

Now, it was time for the second prophecy of Cathbad (that the greatest warrior will die young) to come true. A woman offered Cu Chulainn dog meat. Now, he was stuck in a dilemma. He couldn't refuse the woman because he was not allowed to say no to a lady's hospitality. But, he was also not allowed to eat dog meat.

And yet he had to make a choice. Cu Chulainn chose to consume the dog meat instead of saying no to the lady's hospitality. As soon as he had eaten the meat, his power was negatively impacted. He was not as strong and powerful as before. His days were numbered.

Medb, the Queen of Connacht, attacked Ulster again to steal the stud bull. Cu Chulainn immediately joined the battle on behalf of Ulster. He was only in his early twenties at this time. Cu Chulainn had a vision that confirmed to him his death was near. He saw Morrigan washing his armor, a clear sign that he would die in the upcoming battle. He also realized that this woman was the same one who offered him the dog meat.

Cu Chulainn steeled himself for the worst and raced into the battlefield on his powerful chariot driven by the legendary charioteer, Láeg, and pulled by his favorite steed, Liath Macha. At this moment, Lugaid threw the three magical spears towards the speeding chariot. One of the spears was aimed at Liath Macha, another one at Láeg, and the third one at Cu Chulainn.

Cu Chulainn was a true warrior and did not want to die in a lying-down position. He tied himself to stone so that he would be able to remain standing without falling down even if he was dead. In this standing position, he looked so formidable that no one dared attack him. In fact, no one even came near him for a long time.

It was only when Morrigan, in the form of a raven, took her place on Cu Chulainn's shoulder that Lugaid found the courage to come forward to claim the head of Cu Chulainn. But, a light flashed out from the headless body of Cu Chulainn, and his blade fell from, cutting off the hands of Lugaid. Cu Chulainn had died the death of a hero.

His death was avenged by Conall Cranach, another warrior friend of Cu Chulainn. Conall hunted down Lugaid and killed him before sunset the same day. Even though Cu Chulainn died, Ulster defeated its enemies and emerged victoriously. To this day, Cu Chulainn serves as a symbol of modern Irish nationalism.

Chapter Five:

Other Important Celtic Gods

Danu - the Mother Goddess

The Irish tribe Tuatha de Danann gets its name from Danu, a mysterious mother goddess, and famous ancestor of this tribe. Not much is known about her, although some believe she is connected to the River Danube, the life-giving river in Europe. Others believe that she was the earth or wind goddess who protected her tribe. Let us see what we know about her.

Danu was the Mother Goddess from whom all Irish gods and goddesses descend. Being the mother goddess and the source of all other gods and goddesses, it is believed that she suckled many of the important Celtic deities and allowed them to drink of her mils of wisdom.

All the tribespeople of Tuatha De Danann claim descent from Danu, and she was the source of the tribe's common heritage. Tuatha De Danann gets its power, nobility, and unity from Danu. And yet, Danu remains largely a mysterious deity whom we know very little of.

She was the goddess of power and sovereignty and could grant gifts and boons to nobles, warriors, and kings. All the kings, nobles, warriors, and Ollam drew power from the gifts the mother goddess bestowed on them. The skills and creativity of Tuatha De Danann are believed to be sourced from this mysterious but powerful goddess.

The fact that Tuatha De Danann was a nomadic and migratory tribe, it is believed that Danu could have been either the wind or earth goddess too. Everything and everyone in Ireland depended on her blessings. Her connection to the earth also meant she was the savior and goddess of fairies, fairy mounds, and multiple other dolmens and stones across Ireland.

In some parts of the Celtic world, Danu is worshipped as the river goddess and is believed to have connections with major water bodies across Europe. This connection to water bodies is what drives certain experts to believe that River Danube, one of Europe's longest and greatest rivers, was named after her.

A lot of speculation exists about her, and yet, the one thing that all scholars agree is that all members of Tuatha De Danann were descended from her in one way or another. Kings, noblemen, warriors, craftsmen, judges, tricksters, magicians, poets, and athletes in Tuatha De Danann all came from Danu, the Mother Goddess of the tribe.

Cernunnos

Cernunnos was a Celtic god of the Gauls who associated woodlands, forests, beasts, and all wild places and things. His name itself is an ancient Gaul word for 'horned,' and therefore, he was a horned Gaelic god, and his name is used to refer to other horned gods in Celtic mythology.

He was a mediator between nature and man with the power to tame the wild beings and make human beings understand the importance of the wild for his own. He ruled over the wild, uncivilized parts of the Celtic world. Like Danu, his origins are mysterious as those tales seem to have been lost.

He is known to appear as a bearded man in the company of antlers. He is also often depicted in the center of gatherings consisting of all kinds of wild animals, including elk, snakes, wolves, and aurochs. Such gatherings were possible for Cernunnos because of his ability to bring about peaceful communion even amongst natural enemies. Also, he is shown either wearing or holding a torc, a traditional Celtic necklace.

Brigid

This Irish flame-haired goddess of life, fertility, and spring were referred to as the "Exalted One" as well as the "Goddess of Wells," and often appeared wearing a cloak of a sunbeam. In other European parts of the Celtic world, Brigid was referred to as Brigantes.

She was the goddess of Imbolc, an important Irish winter festival falling on February 1st, marking the start of the new year and the midpoint of winter. Multiple waterways and wells of Ireland are dedicated to Brigid.

Her stories are famous and highly popular all across Ireland. She was the daughter of Dagda and married King Bres with whom she had a son named Ruadan. Ruadan was killed in the Second Battle of Moytura even though he managed to slay Goibhniu, the metalsmith of Tuatha De Danann.

On hearing the news of the death of her son, Brigid rushed to the battlefield to mourn. A loud lament called keening escaped from her lips, and this is believed to be the first feeling sorrow experienced in Ireland. After this, Irish women started the custom of keening at the graves of their loved ones.

Also, the Catholic St. Brigid of Kildare, who is the patron saint of Ireland, shares many similarities with this Celtic goddess. As a Celtic goddess, there are many contradicting attributes given to her.

She was the goddess of healing, motherhood, and fertility, as well as the goddess of fire and passion. Her role of fertility and motherhood was not restrained to the human world but also extended to the animal world. She was regarded as the protector and guardian of domesticated animals.

The following sites in modern-day Ireland represent the popularity of Brigid and her healing and protective powers even today:

- Brigid's Well in County Clare - Located at a church near the Cliffs of Moher, this well is built in a cemetery. The running sound of water is audible, and people still believe in its healing powers.

- Brigid's Well in Kildare - Believed to have the power to heal wounds and illnesses, this well is a famous landmark now dedicated to St. Brigid, although many visitors still come here to worship the Celtic goddess. The Flame of Ireland dedicated to Brigid is located here.

Aengus

Aengus, the Young One, was the son of Dagda and Boann, the goddess of River Boyne. He was also the chief poet of Tuatha de Danann. His poetry and music inspired kings, charmed women, and also helped him to win enemy property from right under their noses. Interestingly, Aengus was himself charmed by Caer Ibormeith, the lady of his dreams whom he married.

Aengus was the god of poetry, love, and youth. Considering these elements overlap naturally with each other makes it easy to understand why Aengus was the god of all three. Not only was he great at art, but he was also cunning and crafty. The combined power of his craftiness and poetry helped him get the better of the elders in his tribe.

Aengus also had the power to resurrect the dead with his breath of life, even if the effect was not permanent. He was a shapeshifter, too, and could easily transform into birds and animals. Also, he could transform gestures of love like kisses into birds and animals too.

The birds and animals that always surrounded him could work as tormentors as well as messengers, depending on Aengus' wishes. Aengus was brought up by his sibling Midir. One of the most popular stories of Aengus is how he collaborated with his father to steal Brú na Bóinne, the home of Elcmar.

The father-son duo visited Elcmar and asked him if they could stay for a day and night. In the ancient Irish language, 'a day and night' could easily be understood as "all days and all nights." Elcmar agreed to their request without thinking and unwittingly ended up giving away his home to Aengus and Dagda forever.

Aengus dreamt of a beautiful girl, and he fell in love with her immediately. His parents tried hard to find the girl of his dreams but to no avail. After years of searching, King Bodg Derg of Munster, a friend of Dagda, located the girl. Aengus went off to get the girl of his dreams.

Aengus found 150 chain-bound women on the banks of a lake called Dragon's Mouth. Aengus was sure that his dream girl was one of these 150 women. However, at the end of that Celtic year or Samhain, these women were cursed to live as swans for an entire year. Aengus struck a deal with the women's captors. He told them that if he could recognize his dream girl as a swan, then they should allow her to marry him.

The captors agreed, thinking that it would be impossible for Aengus in his human form to single out the correct girl from among 150 swans. Of course, they didn't know about the shape-shifting capabilities of Aengus!

When the women turned into swans, Aengus also transformed into one and called out to his dream girl with a song. They found each other and flew away, singing such a beautiful and soothing song that the captors fell asleep for three days.

When he returned home, Aengus found that his father, Dagda, had distributed all his wealth and property to his children, leaving nothing for Aengus. So, he decided to trick his father in the same way both of them tricked Elcmar with the 'a day and night' use of words. Like this, he got sole control over Brú na Bóinne, which he made into his permanent residence.

Ceridwen

Ceridwen is a Welsh white sorceress in possession of a huge cauldron in which she would brew life-changing magical potions, including those that promised beauty, wisdom, and the power to foretell the future in addition to allowing the drinker of the brew to change shapes.

Ceridwen, also spelled in various ways, including Cerridwen, Kerrydwen, or Cerrydwen, is a popular and powerful witch who is blessed with the combined gifts of poetic wisdom, prophecy, and inspiration. These three powers are collectively referred to as Awen in Welsh Celtic mythology. Her magical cauldron and a magical throne both render her with a lot of power.

Ceridwen is married to a powerful Welsh leader Tegid Foel or "Tacitus the Bald" who has his home in Bala Lake or Llyn Tegid. The couple has two children:

- A beautiful girl named Creirwy
- A badly deformed son named Morfran Afaggdu, who has a warped mind and burned skin.

In addition to the above two children, Ceridwen has a third child named Taliesin, which happened through an accident that took place while she was brewing her magical potions. Thanks to the multiple magical gifts passed on by his mother, Taliesin becomes a powerful druid and bard and an advisor to many rulers in Britain. Some experts believe Taliesin to be the precursor of Merlin of Arthurian legends.

Gwydion

Gwydion fab Dôn was an advisor, magician, and mentor to Lleu Llaw Gyffes, his nephew (his sister's son). Gwydion was a defender of the Welsh kingdom, Gywnedd, and also helped his nephew out of trouble many times. Gwydion's magic was as varied as his character and ranged from kindness to malevolence.

Lleu was also a magician who often used his skills to help people around him. However, many of Lleu's tricks frequently had intended and not necessarily happy outcomes in the long-term, and this is where his uncle and father-figure Gwydion came to his help.

In addition to having a sharp mind, Gwydion was also a strong warrior who was able to take on and defeat a powerful Welsh lord in single combat. Gwydion has multiple places in the universe associated with him, including our galaxy, the Milky Way. In the Welsh language, Milky Way is Caer Wydion, which is named after Gwydion's castle.

Arawn

Arawn is the Welsh ruler of the Annwn, a place of blessed and fair afterlife paradise for the Celts, which appeared in Mabinogi. Arawn was a master hunter and a fair and just ruler too. Annwn is described differently in different sources. It is sometimes referred to as an island off the coast of Wales, a kingdom, or a huge cauldron under the sea.

He was a skilled shapeshifter, too, and this capability of his is best demonstrated when he switched his appearance with that of Pwyll, Lord of Dyfed, for an entire year. The switch was so perfect that even Arawn's beloved wife couldn't make out the difference. However, both men remained chaste and did not indulge in lovemaking with the other's wife during the switching period.

Cailleach

Cailleach, an ancient mysterious figure, is found in Welsh and Scottish lore. She was the goddess of old age and winter. Known as the Queen of Winter (she decided the harshness and the length of each winter) and the Veiled One, she helped people living in harsh winters in the north. She was highly popular and prominent right across the Isle of Man, Scotland, and Ireland.

Cailleach is depicted as an old, veiled woman, and usually has one only eye. Her teeth are red, her deathly pale skin is sometimes blue in color, and her clothes are all adorned with skulls. She could ride over storms, leap over mountains, and her shape-shifting skills allowed her to transform into a giant bird.

Interestingly, Cailleach was a gray character, neither completely evil or completely pure and good. While she had a destructive streak in her, she was also highly considerate towards and cared a lot for wild and domestic animals, especially during the harsh winter months. Cailleach was the Winter Queen, and Brigid was the Summer Queen. Some Celts worshipped her as the patron of wolves, and in some parts, she was also a deer herder.

Cailleach was immortal and ageless. According to Manx mythology prevalent in the Isle of Man, Cailleach spent half the year as an old woman and the other half as a young woman. Manx legends refer to her as Cailleach only in her "old woman" version. Many sites in the Celtic regions continue to be relevant to the Celts even today. Some of these places are:

- The Hag's Chair on top of Slieve na Calliagh in County Meath, Ireland

- Hag's Head, at the Cliffs of Moher in County Clare, Ireland

- The whirlpool of the Gulf of Corryvreckan, off Argyll and Bute, Scotland
- Beinn na Caillich, on the Isle of Skye, Scotland
- Ben Cruachan, the largest mountain in Argyll and Bute, Scotland;
- Tigh nan Cailleach ritual site, near Glen Cailleach and Glen Lyon, in Perthshire, Scotland

Nuada

Also, referred to as Nuada, the Silver Hand, he was the first king of Tuatha dé Danann. Nuada was a wise, honest, and just king and very popular among his tribe. However, he had to abdicate his throne because he lost a hand. But, his successor was so cruel and unjust that Nuada was given a silver hand so that he could become king again.

King Nuada set fair and just laws for his subjects and ensured that he himself followed these laws, even when they proved disadvantageous to him. He possessed one of the Four Treasures of Tuatha De Danann, a sword, which no one could defend against or escape from once it was unsheathed.

He lost his hand in the First Battle of Moytura, after which he had to abdicate the throne of Tuatha De Danann to Bres. According to the policy of the tribe, anyone with any blemish was not allowed to be king. Bres was an unjust and unfair ruler. The tribespeople of Tuatha De Danann wanted their old king back. So, they gave him a prosthetic silver hand, after which King Bres was exiled, and Nuada became king again. Later on, he got a flesh-and-blood hand made with magic. Nuada was slain in the Second Battle of Moytura.

Medb

A famed warrior-queen of the Ulster Cycle, Medb reigned over Connacht. Her ambition, skills, and courage put her way many Irish male warriors. Her most famous tale is how she started the Cattle Raid of Cooley to seize the prized bull of Ulster. Her clash with King Conchobar is a famous story in Celtic mythology.

Her strong personality and beauty attracted many suitors to her. However, her strength and power were way above that of many of her suitors. She demanded three things from all her suitors included the absence of fear, jealousy, and mean-ness towards her.

Her first husband was Conchobar mac Nessa, King of Ulster, with whom she had a son named Glaisne. However, both were unhappy in the marriage and were always quarreling with each other. Soon, strong-willed as she was, Medb left her husband's house and went back to her father.

After this, Conchobar married her sister, Ethniu, and was pregnant with his child. During the ninth month of Ethniu's pregnancy, Medb came to Ulster to visit her sister. She killed Ethniu because she was angry with her for marrying her ex-husband. The doctors managed to save the unborn infant (named Furbaide) by performing a cesarean section on Ethniu.

Soon, Mebd became the ruler of Connacht. Conchobar hadn't yet forgiven her for the death of his wife, Ethniu. So, he raped Medb to avenge the murder of Ethniu. It was after this episode that Medb set the three conditions from her future suitors and husbands.

Her nephew and the son of Ethniu, Furbaide, killed Medb when she was bathing in a pool at Inis Cloithreann on Loch Ree.

Badb

Badb, known as the Battle Crow, was one of the three sisters of the Morrigan. Badb sowed discord and fear among combating warriors and had the power to turn the tide of a battle. She was the bringer of death and usually came in the form of an old woman because of which most Celtic experts tend to think that Badb was the old crone form of Morrigan.

Although she caused confusion and created fear on the battlefield, Badb was not pure evil. She had her moments of goodness. She is associated with the present-day banshee, which is rooted in the phrase bean sidhe or "fairy woman." The cries of the banshee signify the announcement or foreboding of oncoming death in the same way the appearance of Badb foretold death during a battle.

Taliesin

Taliesin was known as the Bard of Britons, and he served as an advisory to many Briton kinds, most notably, King Arthur. He was a historian, poet, and strategist in the British Isles. Although many of his tales are legendary, Taliesin did live in the 6th century and was a historical figure to whom legends and myths have been added.

His mythical birth is elaborated in The Tale of Taliesin. He was originally Gwion Bach ap Gwreang, a servant of Ceridwen who was supposed to guard and watch over a special potion that the white witch was brewing for her own deformed son. This potion was really special; only the first three drops rendered the receiver beauty, wisdom, and wit, which was collected referred to as Awen or Awan.

Accidentally, the first three drops fell on Gwion's thumb and burned his skin. Impulsively, he put his thumb into his mouth, and magically he became beautiful, wise, and witty. Ceridwen knew she had lost the most potent three drops. So she chased Gwion in order to kill him.

As he was able to do magic with the same power as Ceridwen, Gwion transformed himself into a hare and ran as fast as he could. Ceridwen transformed into a greyhound and gave chase. Gwion then became a fish, and Ceridwen became an otter to catch him. Again, the fleeing servant transformed himself into a bird, and the white witch became a hawk refusing to give up the chase.

Gwion knew he was at the tether's end. So he transformed into a grain of wheat, and Ceridwen ate up the single grain. Of course, the magic potion Gwion had consumed saved him from death. The single grain became a seed, and Ceridwen became pregnant. She decided to kill the child as soon as he was born. However, she couldn't bring herself to kill her own child, especially a child more beautiful than she had ever seen.

Instead of killing him, she put the baby into a bag of leather-skin and pushed him into the sea. The child was found and rescued by Prince Elffin ap Gwyddno, who named him Taliesin and brought him up as a prince. His soothing-saying skills were first noticed when he visited the court of his foster father's rival, Maelgwn Gwynned, a High King of the Britons.

There, he foretold that Maelgwn would die of Yellow Fever and not on the battlefield. His prediction came true, and after that, his reputation spread far and wide. An increasing number of kings wanted him to be their advisor, and he did play the role of advisor to many Briton kings.

Many more deities, heroes, and warriors adorn Celtic mythology. This book is only a small introduction to the limitless horizon that Celtic mythology offers an interested reader and learner.

Conclusion

Celtic mythology shows marked similarities between Christian Biblical stories and ancient tales of Celtic folklore. While there are varied characters in Celtic mythology, it is primarily filled with kings, warriors, deities, gods, goddesses, magicians, and some powerful animals too.

The characteristics and traits used to describe Celtic deities were often the ones that the Celts wanted to uphold and emulate. These stories were also used as life lessons through tales that taught people what not to do.

Celtic mythology has seen a big revival in the last few decades. Many authors have been inspired by Celtic myths and legends, including J. R. R. Tolkien, who wrote the gigantic "Lord of the Rings" based on his inspirations from Celtic mythology.

There are multiple other modern-day fantasy stories and games inspired by Celtic mythology. Some of them are:

- Dagda appears as the leader of the Celtic pantheon of gods in nearly all the editions of Dungeons & Dragons, a role-playing game.

- Morrigan appears as a powerful triple goddess of Abnormal women in Sanctuary, a Canadian TV series.

- Lugh has appeared in multiple video games in small roles, including in Binding Blades (along with a twin named Llew; the name of his Scottish counterpart), Fire Emblem, and more.

- Brigid of Kildare: A Novel - by Heather Terrell - This book combines the traits of Brigid of Celtic mythology and St. Brigid of Catholics.

- Hounded - by Kevin Hearne - In this book, the main protagonist is Atticus O'Sullivan, the last of the magical Druids. He runs a bookshop on the occult. During his spare time, he uses his shape-shifting skills to transform and go hunting with his Irish wolfhound. Atticus is believed to have been inspired by Aengus.

- Octavia Randolf created the series "The Circle of Ceridwen," where a character by the name of Ceridwen exists, although in a historical setting. The series draws a lot of inspiration from German and Norse myths too.

As already mentioned earlier, this book can only be the tip of an iceberg. The more you read Celtic mythology, the more mysteries and fantasies you will encounter.

References

http://www.mythencyclopedia.com/Ca-Cr/Celtic-Mythology.html

http://www.ireland-information.com/irish-mythology/the-morrigan-irish-legend.html#:~:text=The%20Morrigan%20

https://www.historyextra.com/period/celtic-myths-the-tales-that-might-have-inspired-star-wars-and-harry-potter/

https://www.ancientpages.com/2018/04/07/four-magical-treasures-of-tuatha-de-danann/

https://galaxypress.com/folklore-and-mythology-are-strong-influences-in-modern-fantasy/

https://mythopedia.com/celtic-mythology/gods

Printed in Great Britain
by Amazon